NO LONGER
PROPERTY OF
DENVER PUBLIC
LIBRARY

D1790415

WORLD HISTORY Need to Know

SilverTip

The Industrial Revolution

by Daniel R. Faust
Consultant: Caitlin Krieck, Social Studies Teacher and Instructional Coach, The Lab School of Washington

Minneapolis, Minne:

DENVER PUBLIC LIBRARY

Credits
Cover and title page, © ZU_09/iStock; 5, © alterfalter/Shutterstock; 7, © Culture Club/Getty Images; 9, © Universal History Archive/Getty Images; 11, © Science & Society Picture Library/Getty Images; 13, © SOTK2011/Alamy; 15, © Hulton Archive/Getty Images; 17, © Bestbudbrian/Creative Commons Attribution-Share Alike 3.0; 19, © Print Collector/Getty Images; 21, © Heritage Images/Getty Images; 23, © Archive Photos/Getty Images; 25, © adoc-photos/Getty Images; 27, © Ground Picture/Shutterstock; 28T, © Pixel-Shot/Shutterstock; 28ML, © Oleggg/Shutterstock; 28MR, © muratart/Shutterstock; 28BL, © KANGWANS/Shutterstock; 28BR, © Sergey Bogdanov/Shutterstock.

Bearport Publishing Company Product Development Team
President: Jen Jenson; Director of Product Development: Spencer Brinker; Managing Editor: Allison Juda; Associate Editor: Naomi Reich; Associate Editor: Tiana Tran; Senior Designer: Colin O'Dea; Designer: Elena Klinkner; Designer: Kayla Eggert; Product Development Assistant: Owen Hamlin

A NOTE FROM THE PUBLISHER: Some of the historic photos in this book have been colorized to help readers have a more meaningful and rich experience. The color results are not intended to depict actual historical detail.

STATEMENT ON USAGE OF GENERATIVE ARTIFICIAL INTELLIGENCE
Bearport Publishing remains committed to publishing high-quality nonfiction books. Therefore, we restrict the use of generative AI to ensure accuracy of all text and visual components pertaining to a book's subject. See BearportPublishing.com for details.

Library of Congress Cataloging-in-Publication Data

Names: Faust, Daniel R., author.
Title: The industrial revolution / by Daniel R. Faust.
Description: Silvertip books. | Minneapolis, Minnesota : Bearport
   Publishing Company, [2024] | Series: World history: need to know |
   Includes bibliographical references and index.
Identifiers: LCCN 2023031019 (print) | LCCN 2023031020 (ebook) | ISBN
   9798889165491 (library binding) | ISBN 9798889165569 (paperback) | ISBN
   9798889165620 (ebook)
Subjects: LCSH: Industrial revolution—Juvenile literature. | Economic
   history—Juvenile literature.
Classification: LCC HD2321 .F38 2024 (print) | LCC HD2321 (ebook) | DDC
   330.9/034—dc23/eng/20230727
LC record available at https://lccn.loc.gov/2023031019
LC ebook record available at https://lccn.loc.gov/2023031020

Copyright © 2024 Bearport Publishing Company. All rights reserved. No part of this publication may be reproduced in whole or in part, stored in any retrieval system, or transmitted in any form or by any means, electronic, mechanical, photocopying, recording, or otherwise, without written permission from the publisher.

For more information, write to Bearport Publishing, 5357 Penn Avenue South, Minneapolis, MN 55419.

Contents

Make It Quick. 4
Homemade 6
The First Factories. 10
Powering Change. 14
The Revolution Spreads. 16
Growing Cities, Changing People . . 18
Traveling Out. 22
From Steam to Electricity 24
The New Normal 26

A Revolution Cycle 28
SilverTips for Success 29
Glossary 30
Read More 31
Learn More Online 31
Index 32
About the Author 32

Make It Quick

In today's world, we can bake hundreds of loaves of bread at once. It takes less than a day to put together a car. But making what we want and need hasn't always been this quick. How did we get to this point? It's all thanks to the Industrial Revolution.

> *Industrial* is a word that has to do with work. A revolution is a sudden change. So, the Industrial Revolution describes a sudden change in the way people worked.

Homemade

Before the Industrial Revolution, almost everything was made by hand. People would sew clothes and build furniture. They farmed most of their food.

Many people made most of what they needed. The few things they could not make themselves they bought from people who lived nearby.

Most businesses during this time were run out of small homes, or cottages. People often sold one kind of thing. Now, the term cottage **industry** is used for small **specialty** businesses.

Then, people from Europe started traveling more. They could not get everything they needed as easily when they were away from home. This created a growing **demand** for **goods**, or things to buy, in new places.

As Europeans traveled, they found new things. They came across cotton plants. Europeans found different kinds of wood. Soon, they took these things from other countries. Europeans started selling them.

Cotton became a big crop in Europe and the United States.

The First Factories

The Industrial Revolution began in Great Britain in the 1760s. Business owners wanted to meet the needs of people living in new ways.

They began to change the way things were made. Many built factories. They hired lots of workers. As a group, workers could make things quickly.

Some of the first factories made **textiles**. Suddenly, it was easier for people to buy fabrics. The factories made a lot of money selling their goods. Then, they hired more people. The cycle continued.

Workers in these new factories made things in many small steps. Most workers did only one part of the process. Then, they would pass it to another worker to do the next part. They worked in these **assembly lines** to quickly put together many kinds of goods.

> Workers in an assembly line had to know only their own part in the process. This was easy to teach. Factories could hire people who had not worked before. However, they often paid them less.

Factories often hired women and children.

Powering Change

Machines helped factory workers make things quickly. These machines needed power. The earliest factories were powered by nature. Wind and moving water made their machines work.

Then, people figured out how to use steam for power. The **steam engine** sped along the Industrial Revolution.

> Needing moving water or wind for power limited where factories could be built. Many were next to rivers. With steam power, factories could be anywhere.

Factories burned coal to heat water. The steam then moved parts of engines for power.

The Revolution Spreads

With each new power source and piece of **technology**, the revolution picked up speed. The Industrial Revolution soon spread. Other parts of Europe started building things in factories. It took hold in the United States by the 1790s.

> It took longer for the Industrial Revolution to get to some parts of the world. Many places did not get access to the machines they needed until much later.

Slater Mill in Rhode Island was the first factory in the United States.

Growing Cities, Changing People

As factories grew, their workers needed places to live. Cities spread out around factories. There were homes for factory workers and their families.

Factory workers could no longer farm their own food or spend as much time on other tasks. They bought most of what they needed from shops.

> Inventions from the Industrial Revolution made many jobs faster and easier. However, this put some people, such as farmers, out of work. So, even more people turned to new factories for jobs.

The Industrial Revolution also brought about social change. Before this time, most people were divided into two groups, or classes. One was very rich. The other was poor. The growth of cities created a third. People in a new **middle class** made money working in factories, but they were not rich.

> The growing middle class was important. The workers made many of the things everybody needed. That gave them power. They joined together to fight for better safety on the job. They asked for better pay.

Traveling Out

The same technology that improved factories made it easier for people to live in new places. The steam engine made travel faster. Steamboats took people and goods by river. Railroads were built to go where boats couldn't. People spread out.

> Before railroads, most people had to travel by horse. It could take months to get from New York to California. Steam-powered trains cut that time to just a few days!

From Steam to Electricity

Steam power was just the start. A second wave of the Revolution came in the later half of the 1800s.

Electricity changed things again. It was cleaner and cheaper than steam power. Factories powered by electricity were often faster, too.

Electricity had a huge impact on daily life. It powered factories. It was also used to light up streets at night. Soon, electricity was sent to homes.

Paris, France, had the first electric streetlights.

The New Normal

The Industrial Revolution changed the way people worked and lived. It also made it easier to find cheaper goods. With extra money in the middle class, more people started owning more stuff. The revolution set us on a path that we are still following today.

> Some people say we are in a third wave of the Industrial Revolution. It is focused on technology built around communication. There are many new ways of getting and sending information quickly.

A Revolution Cycle

The Industrial Revolution fed on itself. The more factories grew, the more people worked in factories. This made the Revolution move even faster.

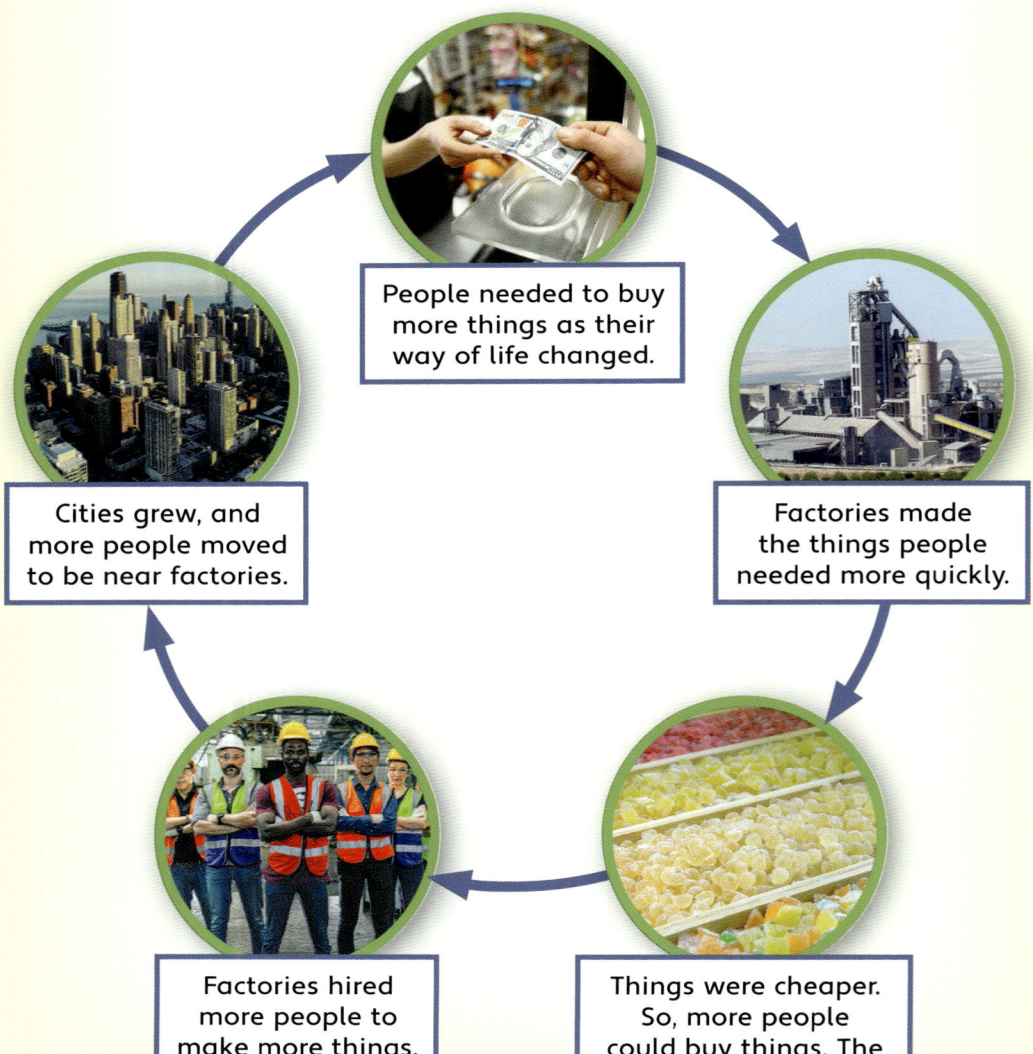

People needed to buy more things as their way of life changed.

Factories made the things people needed more quickly.

Things were cheaper. So, more people could buy things. The factories made money.

Factories hired more people to make more things.

Cities grew, and more people moved to be near factories.

SilverTips for SUCCESS

★ SilverTips for REVIEW

Review what you've learned. Use the text to help you.

Define key terms

assembly lines   steam engine
factories   middle class
Industrial Revolution

Check for understanding

How did people get what they needed before the Industrial Revolution?

Explain how the Industrial Revolution changed the ways people lived.

What spurred the second wave of the Industrial Revolution? How was it different from the first?

Think deeper

In what ways would your life be different if the Industrial Revolution had never happened?

★ SilverTips on TEST-TAKING

- **Make a study plan.** Ask your teacher what the test is going to cover. Then, set aside time to study a little bit every day.

- **Read all the questions carefully.** Be sure you know what is being asked.

- **Skip any questions** you don't know how to answer right away. Mark them and come back later if you have time.

Glossary

assembly lines systems with machines and workers in which work passes from one to the next until the product is finished

demand a need for something

goods things that are made to be bought and sold

industry the businesses or companies that make, sell, or trade things to make money

middle class a group that fills the space between upper and lower classes in society

specialty intended for a specific purpose

steam engine an engine that heats water and uses the steam to move parts

technology useful things made to do work or solve a problem

textiles woven or knit cloths

Read More

Hansen, Grace. *Living through the Industrial Revolution (Living through American History).* Minneapolis: ABDO, 2023.

Lynch, Seth. *The Industrial Revolution (A Look at U.S. History).* New York: Gareth Stevens Publishing, 2019.

Roberts, Russell. *Children in the Industrial Revolution (Children in History).* Mendota Heights, MN: Focus Readers, 2019.

Learn More Online

1. Go to **www.factsurfer.com** or scan the QR code below.
2. Enter "**Industrial Revolution**" into the search box.
3. Click on the cover of this book to see a list of websites.

Index

assembly lines 12
cities 18, 20, 28
demand 8
electricity 24
factories 10, 12–18, 20, 22, 24, 28
goods 8, 10, 12, 22, 26
Great Britain 10
middle class 20, 26
second wave 24
steam 14–15, 22, 24
technology 16, 22, 26
travel 8, 22
United States 9, 16–17

About the Author

Daniel R. Faust is a freelance writer of fiction and nonfiction. He lives in Queens, NY.